—THE GREAT BOOK OF—
BATTLES

RAY ROURKE PUBLISHING COMPANY, INC
WINDERMERE, FLORIDA 32786

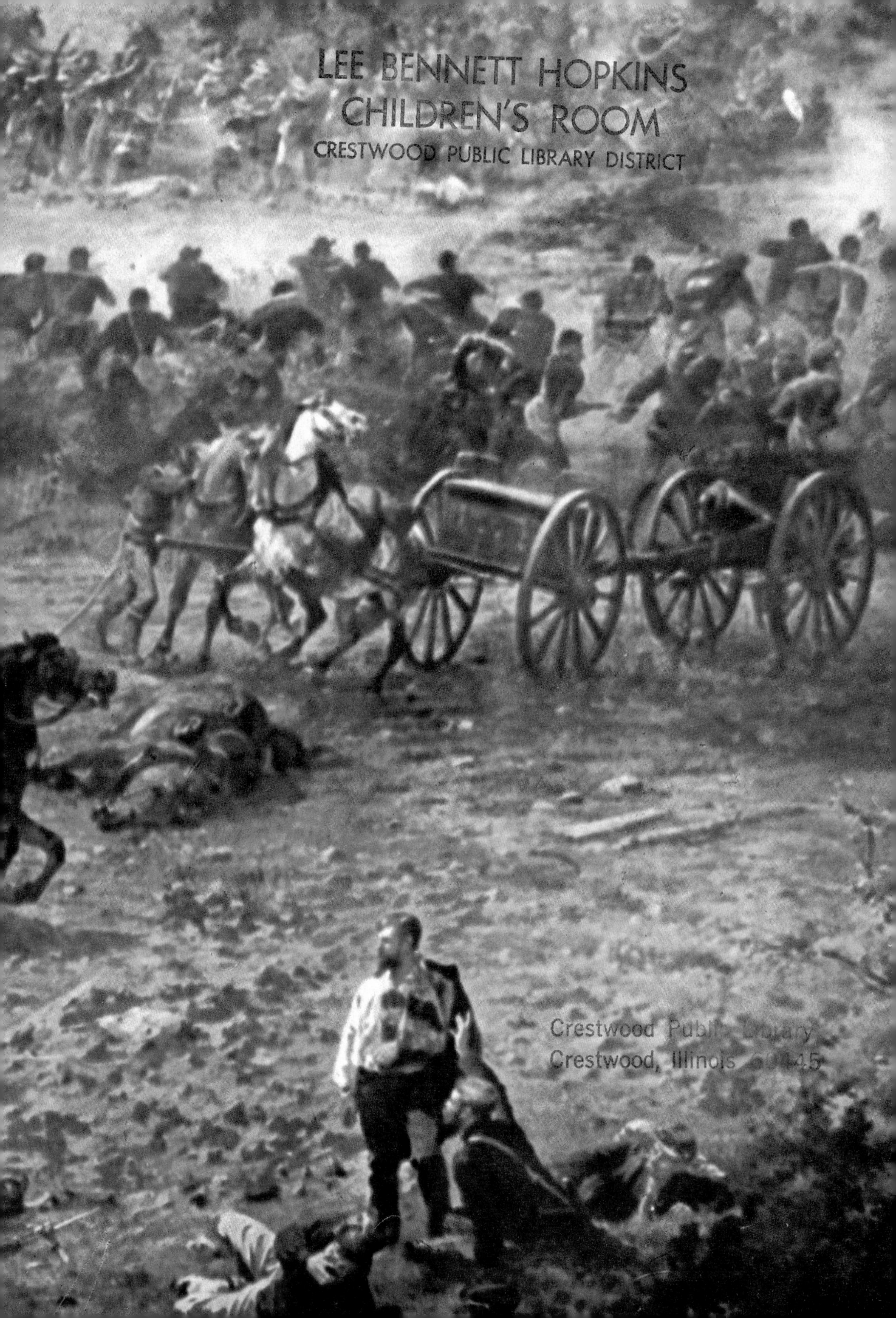

Library of Congress Cataloging in Publication Data

Williams, Brian.
  The great book of battles.

  Includes index.
  SUMMARY: Discusses why and how men have
gone to war in ancient and modern times and
describes some famous battles.
    1. Battles—Juvenile literature.
[1. War.   2. Military history.   3. Battles]
I. Title.   II. Title: Battles.
D25.W544   1981   904'.7   81-11948
ISBN 0-86592-066-4   AACR2

**Right: A modern Swedish self-propelled gun.
Previous pages: An artist's impression of
the Battle of Gettysburg, fought in 1863
during the Civil War.**

**COVER: A British tank from World War I.
Top row of box: Simon Bolivar fighting the
Spanish; air battle in World War I. Center
of box: Napoleon Bonaparte. Bottom of
box: Greek soldiers at the Battle of
Thermopylae; Crusaders.**

—THE GREAT BOOK OF—

BATTLES

RAY ROURKE PUBLISHING COMPANY, INC
WINDERMERE, FLORIDA 32786

Contents

Editorial

Author Brian Williams

Designer Keith Groom

Editor Angela Royston

Published by Ray Rourke Publishing Company, Inc. Windermere, Florida 32786.
Copyright © 1981 Grisewood & Dempsey, Ltd.
Copyright © 1981 Ray Rourke Publishing Company, Inc.

Battles

War and battles are as old as man. Several factors may decide the outcome of a battle. Luck, for example: when King Harold of England was killed by a stray arrow at the Battle of Hastings, his hard-pressed army broke in despair, and history was made. It has been said too that the most successful general is the one with the largest army. But this is not always so, and many famous victories have been won against apparently overwhelming odds.

This book looks at some famous battles—on land, sea and in the air. Each has its own story: of skillful tactics, careful planning, surprise and concealment, grim defense and dashing attack, and very often of muddle and confusion too. The invention of new weapons has helped to win battles, and the arms race has actually been going on for hundreds of years. But more than anything, the story of battle is about courage and determination—the soldier's will to win.

Knight jousting at a tournament

7

Warriors Long Ago

In the heat of battle, many factors can affect the outcome—the skill of a commander, the bravery of his soldiers, the kind of weapons they have, and so on. But time after time, the common soldier has held the key to victory.

The first soldiers were probably also skillful hunters; their weapons were rocks, spears, clubs and slingshots. It was in Mesopotamia, in the Middle East, that the first proper armies appeared. Even then, battles were little more than a series of fights between small groups of warriors, who gathered on the battlefield.

Some 3500 years ago, the Egyptians and Assyrians organized more effective armies. The Egyptians used horse-drawn chariots, and relied on speed to defeat their enemies. Around 1000 BC the Assyrian army was the most feared in the world. It used chariots, cavalry and infantry, and its soldiers were tough and well equipped.

In many respects the first "professional" soldier was the Roman legionary. A legion was a regiment of 5000 men, and the men's discipline and training were so good that for 500 years the Roman army was seldom defeated. The legions fought in Europe,

The Assyrians, with their battering rams, scaling ladders and well-protected archers, were masters of siege warfare.

Battle

Africa and the Middle East, marching swiftly into battle along the excellent roads built by their military engineers.

Most Roman soldiers fought on foot, advancing on the enemy with shields and swords. Their main missiles were arrows which they fired and spears or javelins which they threw. Infantry made up the bulk of most armies until recent times. In the Middle Ages, poorly armed peasants were the "rank and file" soldiers. The "armored corps" of medieval war were knights on horseback, protected by coats of mail and steel plate.

▼ The medieval knight fought on horseback. His chief weapons were the lance, sword, axe and mace. Chain mail was not strong enough to protect the wearer from arrows fired from crossbows, so it was gradually replaced by a complete suit of steel-plated armor.

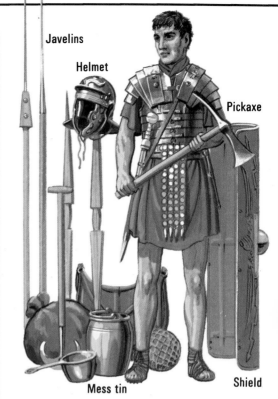

The Roman legionary was armed with two throwing spears or javelins, a short stabbing sword and a shield. He was tough, well trained and versatile.

French armor
1200s

English armor
1300s

German armor
early 1400s

The Warrior's Code

The warrior became a special kind of man, a hero in fact. Tales of brave deeds were very popular, and some religions even encouraged warriors to die in battle. The Vikings believed that dead heroes went to Valhalla to feast with the gods. The Arabs too believed that warriors who fell in battle went to Paradise. Such beliefs made men fearless and scornful of death.

Honor was important to the soldier. Among the Anglo-Saxons, a man was expected to fight and die for his lord. A quarrel between two warriors often led to a blood feud involving their families, friends and servants. Such loyalty gave rise to the important medieval idea of chivalry.

◀ **Knights fought mock battles or jousts, at tournaments.**

The Samurai

These warriors of medieval Japan would kill themselves rather than surrender. They fought on horseback and their favorite weapons were their long swords. Their elaborate and colorful armor protected them and intimidated their enemies. When firearms were introduced they despised them as "cowards weapons".

The samurai formed a proud warrior caste, fanatically loyal to their warlord. Their downfall came, ironically, at the hands of humble foot-soldiers armed with muskets. Not even samurai armor could withstand powder and ball. The samurai's defeat showed that the day of the proud warrior-hero was coming to an end.

The samurai fought for the great warlords of Japan. At the battle of Nagashino in 1575 their wild charges were beaten off by ranks of musketeers.

A medieval knight was supposed to obey the rules of chivalry—to fight bravely in battle, but also show respect for the poor and weak. A boy of noble birth had to train long and hard before becoming a knight. To practice the skills of war, knights took part in mock battles and tournaments.

The rules of chivalry were usually obeyed on the real battlefield. If a knight was captured, he could expect fair treatment and a safe return home (after the payment of a ransom). A wound was far more dangerous than capture. For medical knowledge was so poor that if a wounded man escaped death on the battlefield he was almost certain to die in the clumsy hands of the surgeons.

▶ **A wounded soldier receives medical aid on the battlefield in 1528. Army surgeons were so unskilled that they were little more than butchers.**

Fighting men from three periods in history: left to right: a Swiss musketeer of 1673; an American soldier of the 6th South Carolina Regiment during the American War of Independence; and a French cavalryman of the Napoleonic era. At this time cavalry was the pride of most armies.

Professional Soldiers

New weapons produced a new kind of soldier. He was better trained and better armed than the foot-soldiers of the Middle Ages (who often went to war armed only with pitch-forks and clubs). Gone too were the ponderous armored knights on their heavy horses. By the 1700s only cavalry wore any form of body armor.

Uniforms were slow to develop. At first most regiments were named after the nobles who formed and often led them. When there was no war, the officers went off to hunt while the men returned to their farms. So most troops marched into battle with very little training. Discipline was brutal and pay and food were poor.

During the 1700s, small armies of professional soldiers became common. They wore the brightly colored uniforms of their regiments and armies.

A battle was a confusion of smoke and noise. Commanders seldom had a clear view of what was going on. Troops practiced formal drilling, and marched into line in full view of the enemy before a battle began. Artillery fire was still too slow and inaccurate to do much damage.

In the 1800s weapons became more deadly and armies began to change. Pay, conditions and training improved slowly. Brightly colored uniforms (too easily spotted by snipers) gave way to dull khaki and gray. Most armies remained small until the outbreak of World War I in 1914. Then millions of men were called up to join the fighting.

▲ In 1914, shortly after the outbreak of World War I, the Allied armies halted the German advance at the battle of the Marne. Losses on both sides were huge. The armies dug themselves into trenches, and a new terrible kind of warfare had begun.

▲ During the French Revolution, the French army became a confused mixture of regular troops and raw recruits. However, patriotic fervor inspired the French to victories over the Austrians and Prussians. At the battle of Fleurus in 1794 they even tried using a hot air balloon as an observation post.

▶ Although modern weapons make mass destruction possible, the soldier remains a key factor. Guerillas, living off the land, can win against much superior forces—as was shown in Vietnam. Here the modern weaponry of the United States could not beat a seldom-seen enemy.

Conquering the World

Great

A few remarkable soldiers have made history on the battlefield. Their skill as leaders created empires, and with each victory their fame grew. Hannibal, the great Carthaginian general, was for years Rome's most dangerous foe. Saladin defeated the Crusaders in Palestine, and Genghis Khan ruled the vast Mongol Empire, but most famous of all was Alexander the Great.

In 334 BC Alexander, aged 22, led the Greeks against the might of the Persian Empire. At Gaugamela, in Syria in 331 BC, he defeated a huge Persian army led by King Darius. The Greek phalanxes calmly drew the Persians away from their specially prepared ground. When charged by chariots, the Greeks opened ranks, allowing the

Saladin (1138–1193) led the armies of Islam against the Crusaders. He made himself master of Egypt and Syria and in 1187 captured Jerusalem from the Christians. Not even Richard the Lionheart could wrest the Holy Land from him.

▼ This mosaic, found in the ruins of Pompeii, shows the Battle of Issus in 333 BC. The Persian king Darius flees in his chariot as Alexander (left) approaches on horseback.

Generals

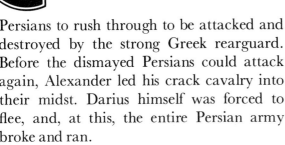

Persians to rush through to be attacked and destroyed by the strong Greek rearguard. Before the dismayed Persians could attack again, Alexander led his crack cavalry into their midst. Darius himself was forced to flee, and, at this, the entire Persian army broke and ran.

Alexander never lost an important battle. He led his army as far as India, and there he wept to find there were "no new worlds to conquer".

The Roman general Scipio with fresh troops and new tactics finally defeated Hannibal. At Zama, south of Carthage, Hannibal lost his last great battle in 202 BC. His war elephants panicked when the Romans blew trumpets and scattered metal spikes in their path.

Genghis Khan

Genghis Khan (1167-1227) was probably the most feared conqueror of all time. His armies swept out of the East as far as Russia. To his victims, who had no idea who the Mongols were, it seemed as if they were being punished by Heaven. They called Genghis the "Wrath of God".

◀ Gustavus Adolphus became king of Sweden in 1611. His troops wore uniforms and his officers had maps (modern ideas for the time). His army was well treated and responded with loyalty and fighting spirit.

Below left: Frederick the Great was a firm but fair ruler. He inherited a strong army from his father and improved its training and discipline until it was the best fighting force in Europe.

▼ Napoleon's genius lay in doing the right thing at the right time. At Austerlitz he knew he must fight, and win, before winter set in. Boldness, timing and the skill of his marshals won him a great victory.

Frederick the Great

Masters of War

Until the 18th century kings often led their armies into battle. Gustavus Adolphus, king of Sweden (1594–1632), organized the most up-to-date army of his age. His musketeers and pikemen fought side by side, protecting each other. They formed up with small cavalry units to make a chessboard pattern. The Swedes' speedy attacks surprised the slow-moving infantry squares of the Catholic League, whom Gustavus defeated at the Battle of Breitenfeld in 1631, shown in the photo on the left.

England's greatest general was the Duke of Marlborough. At Blenheim in 1704, Marlborough and Prince Eugene of Austria defeated the French and Bavarians. First they attacked on the flanks. When the enemy moved troops from his center to meet these attacks, Marlborough's artillery bombarded the weakened positions and then his cavalry smashed through the center of the enemy lines to complete the victory.

Frederick the Great, the warrior-king of Prussia, believed in strict discipline and hard training. During the Seven Years War, the Prussians faced the combined armies of France, Austria and Russia. Yet by fast marching and skillful use of light cannon, they won victory after victory. Frederick's example was admired by an even greater general, Napoleon.

Napoleon had the knack of choosing the right moment to attack. His greatest triumph was at Austerlitz in 1805, when he defeated a larger Russian and Austrian army. By pretending to retreat, Napoleon tempted the enemy to give up a good position on high ground. He stormed their lines with infantry, divided their forces and then turned his cannon on them.

Napoleon Bonaparte

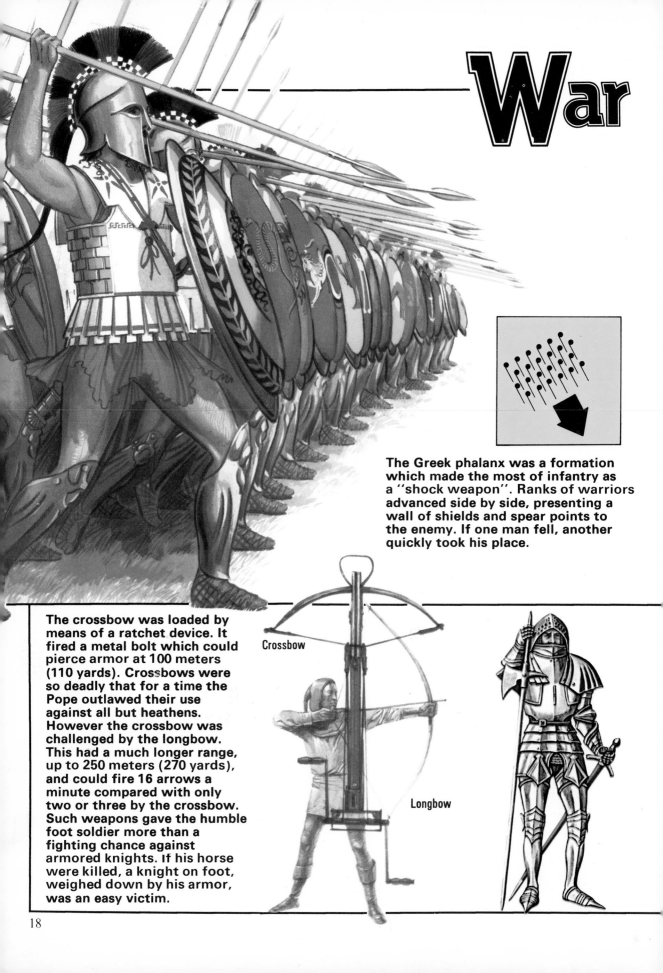

War

The Greek phalanx was a formation which made the most of infantry as a "shock weapon". Ranks of warriors advanced side by side, presenting a wall of shields and spear points to the enemy. If one man fell, another quickly took his place.

Crossbow

Longbow

The crossbow was loaded by means of a ratchet device. It fired a metal bolt which could pierce armor at 100 meters (110 yards). Crossbows were so deadly that for a time the Pope outlawed their use against all but heathens. However the crossbow was challenged by the longbow. This had a much longer range, up to 250 meters (270 yards), and could fire 16 arrows a minute compared with only two or three by the crossbow. Such weapons gave the humble foot soldier more than a fighting chance against armored knights. If his horse were killed, a knight on foot, weighed down by his armor, was an easy victim.

Machines

The Arms Race

A well-trained soldier is the basic "war machine". New weapons give him an added advantage—surprise. The Greeks and Romans did not invent new weapons, but they surprised their enemies by adopting new tactics—fighting in close formation, for example.

The "arms race" for the possession of "super-weapons" is nothing new. During the Middle Ages, archers argued the merits of the crossbow and longbow. Both were good weapons, and a match even for the armored knights who were the "tanks" of the medieval battlefield.

Gunpowder, and the development of muskets and cannon, changed the way battles were fought. Castle walls could not withstand gunfire. Generals were at first slow to see that firearms were the weapons of the future, and that mechanical war was being made possible by science.

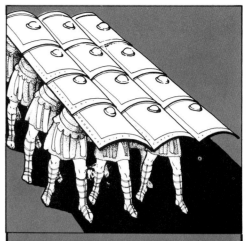

The Testudo

The testudo or "tortoise" was a formation used by Roman soldiers when advancing against enemy fire. Each man raised his shield above his head, locking it against the edges of the shields on either side. The result was an armored "shell" for protection against arrows, spears, rocks and even boiling water. The testudo was a tribute to the Romans' training and discipline, for it must have needed great courage to move forward in this way against a fort manned by barbarian warriors.

Loading a musket

Gustavus, the "father of modern warfare", introduced wheel-lock muskets and light cannon.

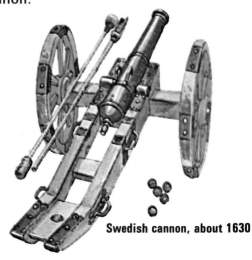

Swedish cannon, about 1630

Attack and Defense

Every new weapon meets its match, for sooner or later attack is countered by defense. Long before gunpowder was known, the Romans used artillery in the shape of giant catapults and crossbows to attack forts. The ancient world also had a mysterious and deadly flame-throwing weapon, known as "Greek fire".

Similar siege engines were used in the Middle Ages to bombard castles, and were probably just as effective as the early cannon. The attackers used scaling ladders and towers to climb over the walls, and dug tunnels under them. A siege might last many months until hunger or sickness forced the defenders to give in. Cannon were frightening and noisy weapons, but they were not accurate or powerful enough to win battles on their own until the 1800s. Then the heavy losses suffered by both sides during the American Civil War showed that troops could no longer advance in the open against quick-firing guns.

However, this lesson was not fully learned until World War I. Unable to advance, whole armies took refuge in trenches. Battles were fought and thousands of soldiers died over a few yards of muddy ground, turned into a wasteland by exploding artillery shells.

Above left: A castle under siege during the Middle Ages. Soldiers are using siege towers and ladders to try and climb over the walls, whilst giant catapults and bombards (early cannon) hurl stones to breach the defences.

▲ A print showing the Duke of Wellington entering Salamanca in Spain during the Peninsular War. In the early 1800s cavalry (dragoons, hussars, lancers and so on) were the most mobile and dashing units.

▶ Canadian infantry defending their trenches against attack at Ypres in 1915. In the bloody fighting of World War I frontal attacks were terribly costly and seldom successful.

Mechanical Warfare

The Italian genius Leonardo da Vinci sketched war machines and even aircraft in the early 1500s. But such ideas remained only dreams until the 1800s and the dawn of the machine age.

Steam power foreshadowed the end of the great sailing warship, although navies were slow to change. The first naval battle between ironclad steamships took place during the Civil War, but the first really "modern" battleship, HMS *Dreadnought*, did not appear until 1906.

Few people thought that aircraft would have any fighting role in war, but during World War I fighter and bomber planes played a growing part. The tank, crawling on caterpillar tracks, also fought in the 1914–1918 War. In the 1940s aircraft and tanks combined in the German "Blitzkrieg" attacks which swept across Europe.

Rapid Fire

This Gatling gun, first used during the American Civil War, had as many as ten barrels which fired in succession as a handle was cranked. The even more deadly Maxim gun of 1884 was the first truly automatic lightweight machine gun. Such weapons were a far cry from the first hand guns, crude cannon mounted on wooden shafts.

▼ The *Holland* (1898) was the first truly seaworthy submarine. Built in the USA it had gasoline engines for surface cruising and electric motors for use under water (like most of its successors).

▲ The first naval battle between ironclads was in 1862 during the American Civil War. *Merrimack* was a wooden frigate converted by the South into an armored ram with ten guns. The North's *Monitor* had two guns mounted in a revolving turret. This duel at sea was indecisive, but showed the shape of things to come.

▶ An aerial "dogfight" between biplanes in World War I. At first, generals could see little use for aircraft (save for spying) and warplanes did not even carry guns. Later, fighter "aces" became national heroes.

Science Goes to War

Gunpowder rockets in China	before 1000
First cannon used in Europe	early 1300s
Matchlock musket in use	by 1500s
Improved flintlock musket	early 1600s
Breech-loading needle gun	1827
Colt revolver	1836
Rifle (range 200 m, 220 yd)	1850
Armored warship	1859
Gatling gun	1863
Maxim machine gun	1884
Holland submarine	1898
Lee Enfield rifle (range 2000 m, 2200 yd)	1902
Dreadnought battleship	1906
First use of tanks	1916
Jet aircraft (He. 178)	1939
Guided missile (V2)	1944
Atomic bomb	1945

▼ Tanks were first used in World War I, but did not come into their own until World War II. More than 1500 tanks took part in the desert battle of Alamein (1942), where conditions were ideal for armored warfare.

The Will

The will to win is a mysterious quality. It explains why David killed Goliath, why Henry V won at Agincourt and why Nelson won at Trafalgar. Great men can inspire their followers to heroism and triumph against apparently overwhelming odds.

Of all the Ancient Greek heroes, one of the most celebrated was Pheidippides, a famous athlete. When the Persians were invading in 490 BC, he ran 240 kilometers (150 miles) to fetch help, fought in the battle of Marathon, and then, without rest, ran to Athens with the first news of the Greek victory. Having gasped his message, he fell dead. But his deed is remembered in the modern marathon race.

Time and again, soldiers have succeeded in turning seemingly inevitable defeat into victory. Weight of numbers does not always guarantee success.

to **Win**

Against All Odds

Salamis

This historic sea battle was fought in 480 BC during the wars between the Greeks and Persians. The mighty Persian fleet of up to 1000 galleys sailed into the narrow strait near the island of Salamis. The Greeks, with some 380 ships, retreated, drawing the Persians after them. Then the Greeks attacked, trying to ram the Persians who, hemmed in by sheer numbers, had no room to turn. In the confusion 200 Persian ships were sunk or captured. The rest fled and never challenged the Greek navy again.

At the Battle of Crecy, the English were led by Edward III and his son, the Black Prince. The victory was won by the skill of the English archers and the greater discipline among the English ranks.

Famous Victories

During the Hundred Years War, English armies won three famous victories over the French: at Crecy (1346), Poitiers (1356) and Agincourt (1415). Each time the English, outnumbered, took up a good defensive position. Their archers' longbows outshot the French crossbows in range and speed of fire. The French bowmen, unable to get close enough to shoot, only got in the way of their knights who were trying to charge the English lines. At Agincourt the weather also helped the English. Heavy rain turned the ground into a quagmire, and many of the heavily armored French men-at-arms were trampled to death.

Freedom Fighters

▲ Yorktown 1781 and the British finally surrender to the American rebels. The War of Independence, begun in 1775, was over. Another 100 years and more were to pass before Canada, Australia, India and the rest of the British Empire became independent too.

▼ Simon Bolivar marched against the Spanish in 1819 with no more than 2500 men. Many died crossing the Andes, but their arrival in New Granada took the Spanish completely by surprise. Bolivar's army won the Battle of Boyaca and entered Bogota in triumph.

Every country has its national heroes, who have fought for freedom when their country was under foreign rule. In the 11th century Rodrigo Diaz (El Cid) fought for Spain against the invading Moors. In France, Joan of Arc was executed in 1431 for her attempts to free her country from English rule. In Switzerland, William Tell inspired his countrymen to oppose the tyrannous Austrian rule.

Some people have become symbols for freedom even beyond their own country. George Washington, who led the American fight for independence from the British, inspired many others. South America was liberated from Spanish rule by two brilliant leaders, Jose de San Martin and Simon Bolivar, who gave his name to the country of Bolivia.

Most freedom fighters use guerilla tactics. Small groups, often working independently, ambush and sabotage the occupying force. Garibaldi was the greatest guerilla fighter of the 1800s, leading the struggle for Italian freedom from the Spanish and Austrians. During World War II, resistance groups fought the German occupation all over Europe.

In recent years many former colonies have gained independence from their European rulers. Some have had to fight to achieve it. In Vietnam, the French were finally driven out by the cunning of Vo Nguyen Giap. Guerilla armies fought in Angola and Mozambique against their Portuguese rulers. In 1979, after years of fighting, the minority white government in Rhodesia gave way to black majority rule.

In 1954 the French tried to lure the Viet Minh guerillas, led by General Giap, into a pitched battle at Dien Bien Phu. The plan misfired. Cut off and surrounded, the French were trapped and after 55 days of fierce fighting, they were overrun.

The Liberators

Three of the most remarkable freedom fighters in history refused to accept honors in reward.

● Joan of Arc (1412–1431) was a peasant girl who inspired the French to unite and defeat the English who had seized much of France. She was burned at the stake by her enemies but her spirit lived on to inspire future generations.

● Simon Bolivar (1783–1830), who was known as "The Liberator" in South America, shunned any other kind of title.

● Giuseppe Garibaldi (1807–1882) led his band of 1000 "redshirts" to free Italy from Austrian rule. When the war was won, and Italy was a united kingdom, Garibaldi retired to the peace and quiet of his farm in the country.

Turning the Tide

Record Battles

● **Bloodiest**
First Somme 1916: more than 1,000,000 casualties.

● **Greatest invasion**
D-Day, 6 June 1944: 1,000,000 men landed within four weeks.

● **Longest siege**
Leningrad: 880 days (August 1941 to January 1944).

● **Largest retreat**
Dunkirk, May 1940: 338,000 Allied troops rescued from France.

● **Longest war**
Hundred Years War, 1346–1453: fought between England and France.

● **Shortest war**
Six-Day War, 5-10 June 1967: between Israelis and Arabs.

The Battle of Gettysburg in 1863 was a turning point in the American Civil War. General Robert E. Lee hoped to invade the North, but this bloody battle (in which both sides lost around 23,000 men) left the Confederate army too weak to do more than retreat into the South.

◄ In the summer of 1812, Napoleon marched into Russia with the largest invasion army Europe had yet seen—450,000 men. As the French advanced, the Russians retreated, burning villages and crops as they went. There was only one full-scale battle, Borodino, before the French reached Moscow. They found the city deserted. No word came from the Czar about surrender, and snow began to fall. With no warm winter clothing and with their supplies running low, the French had no choice but to retreat. The long march home was a nightmare. Thousands died from cold and starvation, or were killed by marauding Russian Cossacks. Fewer than 40,000 survivors reached France.

The Battle of Britain

In the summer of 1940 the German Luftwaffe launched an air attack on Britain. By destroying the Royal Air Force, Germany hoped to prepare the way for a full-scale invasion. A new invention, radar, played an important part in Britain's defenses as waves of German bombers and fighters attacked southern England. The RAF's Hurricanes and Spitfires shot down many of the enemy planes, and finally forced the Germans to abandon their invasion plans.

The Zulus were the most warlike Africans in southern Africa. Their impis (regiments) terrorized other tribes. In 1879 a Zulu force surprised a British army camp at Isandhlwana in Natal. The British had failed to protect the camp properly and were overrun. After this victory, the Zulus moved on to attack a small post known as Rorke's Drift. No more than eighty fit soldiers manned the post, with some thirty or so sick and wounded men. Nevertheless, with the aid of guns, the tiny garrison fought off the Zulus in fierce hand-to-hand fighting.

Battles of Conquest

▲ Before the Battle of Hastings, the English had marched north to repel an invading army from Norway. They then hurried south at the news that William and his Norman army had landed in the south. Harold at once sought battle. The English fought on foot, with axes and spears, but the Normans had brought horses across the Channel. The English "shield wall" held fast on Senlac Hill until the Normans pretended to retreat. Sensing victory, the English broke ranks and pursued them. When the Normans turned and counter-attacked, many English were killed and the battle swung in William's favor.

Makers

The course of history has sometimes been decided by a single battle. Had the English, and not the Normans, won the Battle of Hastings in 1066, English history might have been very different. Like many important battles, Hastings was lost by a combination of bad tactics and bad luck.

The English king, Harold, made a mistake in rushing into battle too soon. At the height of the battle, the Normans tricked the English into leaving their strong hilltop position. Finally, luck played its part when Harold himself was killed. Without its leader, the English army lost heart and was scattered.

Bold conquerors have often been favored by fortune. Genghis Khan, Tamerlane and Babur all won empires in the East through victories on the battlefield. But defenders have also been fortunate—as when the English fleet humbled the mighty Armada in 1588.

The Crusades

For 200 years Christians and Moslems fought for possession of the Holy Land (Palestine). In the 11th century the warlike Seljuk Moslems refused to allow Christian pilgrims to go there. Encouraged by the Church, the Christian kings of Europe led a series of expeditions or crusades to take the Holy Land. In all there were seven, but only the first in 1096 was successful. Later the Christians spent more time quarreling among themselves than fighting the Moslems. In 1187 Saladin recaptured Jerusalem and, although the Crusaders held the stronghold of Acre until 1291, they never again managed to wrest the Holy Land from Moslem rule.

◀ The Moghul Empire, which dominated India for 300 years, was founded by Babur (1483-1530). He was descended from two earlier conquerors, Tamerlane and Genghis Khan. With a tiny army of only 300 tribesmen, the young Babur captured Kabul in Afghanistan in 1504 and invaded India. In 1526 his army fought a great battle at Panipat against the Sultan Ibrahim, who had raised an army four times the size of Babur's. However, Babur had skilled artillery and musketeers, and he positioned his guns behind a barricade of carts. The gunfire terrified Ibrahim's elephants and at the end of the battle 20,000 of his men lay dead.

▲ The Spanish Armada was an invasion fleet of 130 great galleons, packed with troops. For a week, it fought a running battle in the Channel against the English, whose ships were smaller but better armed and faster. When the Armada anchored off Calais, the English sent in fireships to drive it out to sea again. Those Spanish ships that escaped the English guns fled into the North Sea. Many of the survivors were sunk in fierce gales as they tried to sail home round the treacherous coasts of Scotland and Ireland.

▶ Three scenes from the Battle of Blenheim, 1704. Left: English infantry advance across the Nebel River. Center: A brigade of French foot soldiers, abandoned by their cavalry, are cut down. Right: Prince Eugene's Austrians press home the Allied attack on the French flank. Marlborough's plan of campaign meant risking his entire army by marching from the Netherlands into Southern Germany. His victory over the French and Bavarians at Blenheim saved the Austrian capital, Vienna, and thwarted French ambitions of controlling all Europe.

Struggle for Power

The "balance of power" has shifted uneasily throughout history, as nations and sometimes religions have struggled for supremacy. In the early Middle Ages, the religion of Islam swept through Arabia. The followers of the prophet Mohammed believed in "holy war", and this rising tide of Islam brought East and West into conflict—in Spain, in the Holy Land, and in what remained of the old Roman Empire.

The capital of the eastern Roman Empire was Constantinople. When it fell to the Turks in 1453, the long reign of the Byzantine emperors was ended. In Europe religious quarrels caused long and bitter wars, such as the Thirty Years War (1618–1648) in Germany. For many years, too, Catholic Spain and Protestant England were enemies.

The defeat of the Spanish Armada in 1588 saved England from invasion.

The struggle for supremacy in Europe often involved France, particularly during the reign of Louis XIV (1643–1715). He wanted to rule all Europe. During the War of the Spanish Succession, England, Holland and Austria joined forces against France. The Allied commander was the great Duke of Marlborough, who believed the key to victory was attack. Marlborough trained his infantry to fire musket volleys before advancing with bayonets fixed. Cavalry rammed home the attack, charging with swords drawn. With these tactics and Marlborough's bold plan of campaign, the Allies won at Blenheim in 1704 and foiled the French king's ambitions.

The World at War

On December 7, 1941, nearly 200 Japanese planes, launched from aircraft carriers, made a surprise attack on the US naval base of Pearl Harbor, Hawaii. Three battleships were destroyed and others badly damaged. But the Japanese missed the US carriers, which were at sea. The raid brought the United States into World War II. And it was carriers, not out-of-date battleships, that won the naval battles fought in the Pacific.

Until modern times, most wars were local, hence their names: the Afghan War, the Zulu War, the Ashanti War and so on. Often quite small numbers of fighting men were involved. It is true that wars often lasted many years. For a hundred years in the Middle Ages, England and France were at war. But, generally speaking, ordinary people could manage to stay clear of the battlefields, and life went on more or less normally.

The most bitter war is probably civil war, in which opposing factions within a country fight for power. The English Civil War (1642–1652) is an example. However, this war was nothing like so bloody as the American Civil War (1861–1865). Weapons had become much more deadly and, so desperate were the battles, it was often difficult to decide if either side had really won any kind of victory.

World War I (1914–1918) started in Europe and was mostly fought there, although fighting spread to the Middle East and East Africa. For the first time submarines attacked merchant shipping. This meant that even countries not engaged in the fighting also suffered. For the first time, too, towns and cities were bombed from the air by airships and airplanes. So many men were fighting at "the front", that women took over the production of vital supplies.

World War I was called "the war to end wars". But from 1939 to 1945 the world went to war again. In World War II few parts of the globe were far from the fighting. Millions of civilians were killed or became refugees. Armies fought across Europe and in Asia, while the naval war was fought in the Atlantic and Pacific oceans. Machines, notably tanks and aircraft, dominated the fighting. The close of World War II saw the first long range rocket weapons—the German V1 flying bomb and V2 rocket—and, finally, the appalling atom bombs which were dropped on Japan in 1945.

▲ Russian peasants flee from the German advance on Moscow. World War II involved civilians as much as it did soldiers.

▲ Aircraft carriers played an important part in the war at sea.

After more than two years' preparation, Allied soldiers, under the combined command of General Eisenhower, landed on the Normandy beaches on D-Day, 6 June 1944. Within the first week, more than 325,000 men, 50,000 vehicles and 100,000 tons of equipment poured into France. But it took almost another year of bitter fighting before the war in Europe came to an end.

Some Other Famous Battles

Persians defeated Greeks	480 BC	Thermopylae
Hannibal defeated Romans	216 BC	Cannae
Octavius defeated Anthony and Cleopatra	31 BC	Actium (sea)
German tribesmen defeated Romans	9 BC	Teutoberg Forest
Franks defeated Arabs	732 AD	Tours (Poitiers)
Emperor Otto defeated invading Magyars	955	Lechfeld
Christians defeated Turks	1571	Lepanto (sea)
Russians defeated Swedes	1709	Poltava
British defeated French	1759	Quebec
British defeated French and Spanish	1805	Trafalgar (sea)
Allies defeated French	1813	Leipzig
Texans' heroic defence defeated by Mexicans	1836	Alamo
Britain, France, Turkey beat Russians	1854	Balaclava
Prussians defeated French	1870	Sedan
Sioux Indians defeated US army	1876	Little Big Horn
Japanese defeated Russians	1905	Tsushima (sea)
Germans defeated Russians	1914	Tannenberg
British v Germans (draw)	1916	Jutland (sea)
US defeated Japanese	1942	Midway (sea)
Russians defeated Germans	1942	Stalingrad
US defeated North Koreans	1950	Inchon

Persian spearman
500 BC

English archer
1350

Danish
guardsman
1640

Prussian
foot soldier
1750

FOOT SOLDIERS THROUGH THE AGES

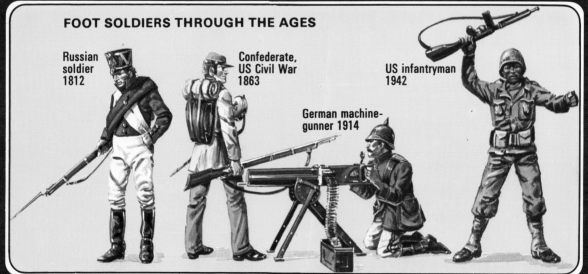

Russian
soldier
1812

Confederate,
US Civil War
1863

US infantryman
1942

German machine-
gunner 1914

Index

Acknowledgements

Cover National Portrait Gallery *center;* Endpapers Gettysburg National Military Park, 10 Victoria
and Albert Museum; 11 Mary Evans; 13 Imperial War Museum *top,* Science Museum *center;*
Associated Press *bottom;* 14 Scala; 16 Musée de la Ville de Strasbourg *top,* Mansell *bottom;* 16/17
Bibliothèque Nationale, 17 National Portrait Gallery; 27 Mansell *top,* National Army Museum
bottom; 22 Radio Times Hulton Picture Library *top* and *center,* Mary Evans *bottom;* 23 Imperial
War Museum; 25 Bodleian Library, 27 Paris Match; 28 Bulloz Musée de l'Armee *top,* Gettysburg
National Military Park *bottom;* 33 National Army Museum; 35 Novosti *top,* Imperial War Museum.

Picture research: Penny Warn.